PEOPLE AND POWER

PEOPLE AND POWER
PORTRAITS FROM THE FEDERAL VILLAGE

PHOTOGRAPHS BY

MICHAEL EVANS

Preface by
GEORGE F. WILL

Essays by
JANE LIVINGSTON
Associate Director and Chief Curator, Corcoran Gallery of Art
and
ALAN FERN
Director, National Portrait Gallery, Smithsonian Institution

HARRY N. ABRAMS, INC.
PUBLISHERS, NEW YORK

Publication of this book coincides with an exhibition
of THE PORTRAIT PROJECT at the Corcoran Gallery of Art,
Washington, D.C., January 12–February 24, 1985

The photograph of Michael Evans on page 222 is by Tom Zimberoff

Project Editor: Robert Morton
Assistant Editor: Beverly Fazio
Designer: Judith Michael

Library of Congress Catalog Card Number: 84–72239
ISBN 0–8109–1481–6

Printed and bound in Japan

CONTENTS

8

GEORGE FREDERICK WILL
Syndicated Columnist

PREFACE

What we have here is a class picture. It is a picture of the ruling class. Or, if you prefer a slightly—but only slightly—less jarring term, it is a picture of the governing class.

Now, I know I have just used inflammatory phrases. The mere mention of "class" jars the Jeffersonian sensibilities of most Americans. What is our "errand into the wilderness" about if not escape from the social deficiencies of the Old World, the foremost of which were class structures? The idea of a governing class in our democracy is considered a contradiction in terms. Do we not enjoy government of and by the people?

Well, as a matter of fact, we do not. Most of "the people" are altogether too busy, not to mention too far away from the seat of power, to rule a continental nation that has a strong central government. Anyway, this is a republic, and the core principle of republicanism is representation, according to which "the people" do not decide issues, they decide who will decide.

That is putting the elementary truth as baldly as possible. However, that truth is not alarming, for a reason that can be read in this volume. The federal government is a collection of individuals, identifiable individuals. And the process of governance, which involves much more than the particular institutions of government, involves many more groups and institutions and individuals, some of whom appear in this collective class picture. Governance involves the communications apparatus (journalism in all its many and multiplying forms), the pressure apparatus (interest groups—in a word, lobbyists), and the cultural apparatus that leavens a great capital.

John Kennedy called Washington a city of northern charm and southern efficiency. That remark certainly was amusing; not very long ago it may even have been true. But it is a dated witticism. Sometime after Kennedy's truncated presidency—perhaps the emblematic moment was the opening in 1971 of something bearing his name, the John F. Kennedy Center for the Performing Arts—Washington reached the critical mass necessary for a great city. By critical mass I mean more, much more, than population. I mean a certain richness in the social texture.

In a moment of exasperation, occasioned by some trifle now long forgotten, I wrote that Washington was like a small town dependent on a large textile mill, a town that knows only about, and not all that much about, textiles. That was unfair (to textile towns as well as Washington) when I wrote it, and is much more so today. Of a sudden, Washington has acquired the sort of competing elites—commercial, financial, intellectual—that enrich the life of any great metropolis.

How suddenly has Washington come of age? Permit me some personal observations which, although anecdotal, are, I think, telling.

When I moved to Washington in 1970, the area on the Mall that now contains the Constitution Gardens was still covered by an unsightly residue of the Second World War—temporary buildings used by the Navy. Relatively recently this clutter of wartime growth was tidied up.

I live in Chevy Chase Village, Maryland, a small incorporated area flush with a small part of the northern line of the District of Columbia and extending a short way along Connecticut Avenue. A portion of the house I live in was built in 1901, when it was a small cottage. It was a rural retreat where the owner could come by carriage to take the country breezes on a height overlooking the city. But this house is just six miles from the White House. Now, of course, it is at the inner core of a sprawling metropolitan area. It is about a mile from the commercial area where the District and Maryland meet, at the intersection of Wisconsin and Western Avenues. That spot is now a congregation of famous retailers—Saks Fifth Avenue, Lord & Taylor, Neiman-Marcus, Brooks Brothers, Cartier, Gucci. But when John Kennedy came to the Senate in 1953, this was a wooded area where trolley cars reached the end of the line and deposited picnickers.

What Washington also now has, not coincidentally, is a governing class. This group is "conspicuous Washington," composed of not more and probably a lot fewer than five thousand persons. Like any living organism, this compact body politic is constantly changing. It is said that over a span of seven years every cell in the human body changes. The renewal of "conspicuous Washington" does not proceed at quite such a brisk pace, for which we should be thankful. After all, the skills of governance are slowly acquired; governance is not an amateur sport. Writing laws, enforcing them, conducting oversight and rulemaking, diplomacy and working to influence or explain all these things—each of these is a profession, long in the learning.

The practitioners in Washington are at the top of a steep social pyramid.

But what matters for the health of a society is that there be some circulation of elites. There certainly is in Washington. The portraits in this book, considered together, are a snapshot, freezing a moment in a process of endless movement. In the year 2000, how many persons here will still be active players in the game of governance? I would guess fewer than half—probably a lot fewer.

In *Phineas Finn* Anthony Trollope describes some politicians entering a room: "At first sight they seemed to be as ordinary gentlemen as you shall meet anywhere about Pall Mall on an afternoon. There was nothing about their outward appearance of the august wiggery of statecraft, nothing of the ponderous dignity of ministerial position." And we may be sure that they seemed the same on second sight, and third, and fourth. Representative governments are, well, awfully representative, at least in this sense: they are made up of folks who look like, and are like, most other folks. There are no distancing, distinguishing uniforms. But the portraits herein reveal more than the democracy of dress. They testify, I think, to democracy's pleasantness.

Consider, for example, the photograph on page 111, the last portrait taken of Senator Henry Jackson, who died shortly afterward. For this portrait Jackson did not bother to get his trousers freshly pressed. That was part of the considerable charm of the fellow who, looking more like Tom Sawyer than Julius Caesar—about as American as it is possible to look—stands there, ten miles short of any pretense, his hands in his pockets, turning toward the camera an unforced smile of the sort that shone on his constituents for several generations. Look long and hard at this picture of one of the half-dozen greatest Senators of all time, and ask yourself: is there anything about it that gives even the slightest hint that this man, more perhaps than any in our time, was a complete professional at the use of power?

Jackson came to Congress six months before I was born and participated in all the events that transformed Washington into a complex collection of professions. Geologists take core samples, drilling down through the layers of the earth. This collection of photographs is a social core, a slice of the geology of governance in late-twentieth-century Washington. As you turn these pages, remember the British diplomat Canning's advice: "Away with the cant of measures, not men!—the idle supposition that it is the harness and not the horses that draw the chariot along." It is your chariot; in fact, you are in it.

GEORGE F. WILL

11

JANE S. LIVINGSTON
Associate Director and Chief Curator, Corcoran Gallery of Art

THE ART AND ARTLESSNESS
OF THE PORTRAIT PROJECT

These photographs by Michael Evans of people circulating through the channels of political influence in the nation's capital comprise a virtually unprecedented body of images. Formal portraits they are not. Neither are they strictly photographic documents, nor candid subjective impressions, nor straight identity shots. Taken together they make a strange multi-faced record, a rich yet uninflected panorama of a rarefied stratum of American society in one short time span.

To photograph so austerely as Evans does, so ruthlessly as to purge gesture, landscape, and interior detail from every one of more than five hundred images, is to engage in a prolonged enslavement to work that is basically mechanical. This (unacknowledged) drudgery is in the nature of Evans's procedure. It began and it ended as an extended labor disguised as an experiment, this ostensibly simple recording of personages invited to the artist's Washington, D.C., studio. All during the amassing of this body of pictures, the artist was fulfilling his official duties as Personal Photographer to the President of the United States and head of the White House photographic staff: he was traveling with the presidential entourage, covering every official event in and out of the home base, executing and overseeing all the photographic documentation routinely carried out in the course of an American presidency. That he was able to fulfill the Portrait Project at all is remarkable; that it is so consistently craftsmanlike is astounding. It is interesting to contemplate its sheer requirement of concentration, or rather the bifurcated concentrations needed to drive the undertaking steadily during four years.

Each picture generally works well in its own right. But it is probably on the cumulative level that the photographs assume their most arresting and important identity. For collectively these images of men and women—distinguished one from the other by subtle, sometimes nearly indiscernible particularities—communicate worlds of truth about our time. They bespeak a poignantly specific character of being which reverberates in our nation's governmental persona: they show us in depth one of the fluctuating casts of historic players. This is a pageant without artifice, irony, or drama—without, in short, any strong authorial viewpoint. The images radiate a stark, if fully dressed, human presence, free from background. Evans isolates his subjects from their contexts: he refuses to entertain us with his own skill, while refusing equally to let his subjects seduce us with whatever expressive power they may command.

The photographer from the beginning seems to have wanted in this undertaking to penetrate to some deeper-than-journalistic view. Without probing, he aimed for some new quality of insight. But he let this unfold without manipulating his subjects. People deliberately facing the camera do display themselves, which is not to say they necessarily reveal themselves. Often, in even the most impersonal photo session, personages communicate surprising aspects of character which we feel could not possibly have been consciously intended, though for the most part, people in the public eye maintain a certain inscrutability before the lens.

The usual relationships between the leading portrait photographers of our time—Yousuf Karsh, Arnold Newman, Richard Avedon—and their subjects is by definition freighted with collusion. An implicit reciprocity generally exists in any posed photograph, especially when a skilled author faces a notable subject: this mutuality, and an acute concomitant style-consciousness, has become the very essence of most recent portraiture. Michael Evans's Portrait Project goes against this now-familiar dynamic of exchanged narcissism, this artist-to-subject congratulatory pact. Evans's approach simply doesn't allow for the overt injection of ego: his subjects are therefore (though unwittingly) freed in the momentary act of representation.

The danger, of course, in such an audacious act of unmitigated artlessness as is committed in Evans's exhaustive recording lies in its potential to produce an *oeuvre* of monumental banality. The photos might simply bore us to desperation. Which observer, conditioned by the various seductions and quick-hit stimulation of so much contemporary journalistic and art photography, is prepared really to attend to this immense body of images, each so similar to the other and each so apparently neutral? Can we really expect to be diverted by seeing this peculiar array of more or less deadpan, insistently nongestural, unglamorous, nonsatirical, essentially *affectless* portraits? The surprising answer, I think, is that we do indeed find ourselves if not exactly entertained in the process of studying these photographs at least strangely absorbed. There is a mysterious fascination first in simply seeing, then in trying to identify each sitter; and then in scrutinizing, speculating about, or simply observing details we would not otherwise notice in these people, or

14

indeed any of the characters who inhabit our familiar political environment.

We take for granted what is shown to us every day, what thus becomes part of our projected selves: only the anomalous character in our midst ordinarily captures our objective scrutiny. Freaks or renegades separate themselves from the background, as do those other human beings who incite in us strong feelings of competition or identification through similarity of sex, age, or role. To underscore this point, one has only to consider the power of lapsed time to alter our capacity for objective perception of photographs and our consequent interest in them. The same snapshots of uniformed soldiers returning home from Austria or France in 1944 and reuniting with their wide-shouldered, stiffly coiffed wives or lovers, which were virtually invisible as objects of cultural significance to their contemporaries, are already—merely forty years later—strikingly evocative and occasionally moving beyond reason. Even more to the point, those calculatedly "typical" photographs of bourgeois or working-class Germans documented by August Sander in the early years of this century might have seemed—*must* have seemed—to their contemporaries somewhat opaque (if unusually powerful in their framing and directness) and somewhat ordinary. Now, of course—partly by virtue of their stylistic and cultural particularities, those subtle details of dress or gesture that date them and place them—they virtually palpitate with spirit and meaning for the contemporary viewer. Sander's consummate, perhaps unique, capacity to capture these ordinary subjects and transform them into works of art has been powerfully enhanced by the passage of time.

To compare Evans with Sander is perhaps to overstate the former's importance either for ourselves as audience of his present body of work, or for those in future generations who may encounter his record of a powerful segment of a society in an historically ascendant geopolitical position. It is, however, incontrovertible that even today this odd body of work somehow asserts a notable aura of integrity, an arrestingness. It has stature as art in spite of its simplicity and the startling absence of sophistication with which it was carried out. We might even say that Michael Evans is a genuine naif in the context of international art photography and that his sudden entry into the field is a kind of whimsically conspired-to fluke, the result of a few individuals responding to the accident of his being in this place at this time and of his having a kind of mad surplus of energy and dogged persistence. But to say this would be to ignore or deny the staying power of the photographs themselves in their capacity to hold their own against the most rigorous and skeptical evaluation, to keep affecting us after weeks, months of repeated viewing.

Without being profoundly expressive or insightful, the photographs carry an uncanny integrity of characterization. We feel in the end their accumulated power of simple, unburdened reality, a relaxed and yet ever so slightly self-conscious quality of subjects responding to an unportentous experience. For Evans brought to his brief sittings neither the elaborate appurtenances of the impresario portraitist's studio nor its inevitably theatrical atmosphere. He brought simply his own polite, slightly distracted, low-keyed, deceptively off-hand self to the encounter: he literally disarmed his subjects, while insisting upon a distance that insured the preservation of his subjects' self-possession. Quite naturally, his subjects may have been slightly nervous, imperceptibly wary, impatient, curious, or perfunctory in their attitudes. But they virtually never surrendered to a condition of either intensity or relaxation that might have catalyzed the kind of defenseless revelations we associate with other contemporary portraitists.

Perhaps this odd combination of casualness and distancing, occurring both between the photographer and subject in the act of recording and in the viewer's perception of the pictures, is a distinctively post-modern characteristic. It is difficult to imagine quite the degree of calculated nonportentousness or the shared sense of remoteness being evoked in any series of portraits by Nadar, Mathew Brady, or, for that matter, August Sander. Evans has somehow managed to shed the normal associations with "art photography" that nearly every other portraitist somehow communicates, willingly or not. Just as the subjects he has chosen are usually abstracted from both art and symbolic life dramas—preoccupied more with professional endeavor than with a simple state of being and unconcerned in the act of presenting themselves before the camera—so the photographer has become correspondingly outer-directed, sublimating the usual interpretive or creative drives in the name of a higher collaborative neutrality. These are characteristics not only of this project, but of much of the nonphotographic art of our time.

Apart from participating in the esthetic tendencies of his moment, Evans conveys—I think unintentionally—a startling truth of our present society. It is a message we may not be prepared to accept, a notice of our essential conformity. Our leaders, and perhaps by implication ourselves as a society, certainly portray distinctive attributes. But one experiences an odd sensation in scrutinizing these images: their subjects so often lack the intensity of individuated character, participating both in role-determined stereotypes and in socially conditioned expressions of feature. Indeed the subtle homogeneity among both the bureaucrats and the interpreters of our time in this nation could scarcely be more ruthlessly or incontrovertibly shown than in these portraits. For they expose as much as they respectfully withhold: their power lies sometimes in their very coldness, sometimes in their candor, often in their gentleness and reserve.

Evidently we are no longer a nation whose every class harbors eccentricity, as was surely true in recent generations. On the contrary, these images seem to be telling us, our outward demeanor bespeaks the presence of conventions of dress, facial expression, bodily posture, set of gaze, or angle of head. The shared language of our physical self-presentation exerts itself clearly in the eye of Michael Evans's camera.

JANE LIVINGSTON

18

ALAN FERN
Director, National Portrait Gallery, Smithsonian Institution

PORTRAITS:
IMPERIAL, OFFICIAL, AND PERSONAL

The photographs of Washington notables by Michael Evans have an inescapable, almost hypnotic, fascination. We find ourselves comparing our impressions—gleaned from news stories—of presidential advisors or legislators with our reading of these portraits, in which the language of face or stance confirms or denies our previous attitudes.

The impulse to record the images of government leaders seems to be as old as government itself. People have always felt a need to know what their rulers looked like, and, except in those cultures that proscribed the making of images, have used effigies of those rulers to celebrate the triumphs of their states. As rulers succeeded one another, these celebratory portraits began to form themselves into groups.

Of course the busts, standing figures, and equestrian monuments in, say, a Roman town square had little to do with the expression of the human side of the emperors and the leading citizens. Instead, they were expressions of the state portrait's power to arouse patriotic fervor and to recall the glories of previous administrations. Related as they were in both form and style, these portraits spoke of the collective strength and nobility of the power structure of the empire. Portraits on coins, the parades of saints and kings on the facades of the medieval cathedrals, and—with the advent of printing—the albums of woodcut or engraved portraits of religious and political leaders constitute a rich legacy of serial portraiture in Western civilization.

In coinage, public sculpture, and the graphic arts the political portrait tended to be idealized and generalized. Little attempt was made to show the public person in a private role. The emperor did not put aside his robes or the bishop doff his mitre so that the sculptor or engraver could show him as he "really" was. On the contrary, these persons were little known apart from the positions they held; no matter how individual the king's features might be, he would not really be recognized without his crown, robes, and mace.

With the advent of the sixteenth and seventeenth centuries, painters' attitudes toward the portrait began to change. Merchants, poets, seafarers, philosophers, and, later, even ordinary citizens sat for their portraits. Now the artist and his audience became fascinated with capturing a likeness, and with

19

exploring the psychological reality of the human being behind the likeness. It is hard for us today to know the backgrounds of Rembrandt's subjects, for example, but their human qualities are immediately accessible. Even in Rembrandt's time idealized portraits existed side by side with the psychologically more interesting portraits of ordinary men and women. Books were published that gathered together engraved portraits of worthy public figures, often rendered in uniform size and with standard borders. These were the first galleries of portraits, and the passion for these collections endured.

When, in the 1780s, Charles Willson Peale painted the portraits of the men who had played important roles in the American Revolution and in the establishment of the United States of America, he was creating works that "might be valuable in a future day." The portraitists of the Age of Enlightenment and their successors in the early nineteenth century regarded the collection of notable portraits as having a moral and educational role: inspiring future generations by the example of the past. In their preface to *The National Portrait Gallery of Distinguished Americans*, finished in 1839, James B. Longacre and James Herring wrote that they were creating "a monument of national gratitude and the evidence of a just appreciation of the brave, the honorable, and virtuous achievements which indicate to the world the high destiny of the republic."

The invention and refinement of photography in the 1820s and 30s soon brought portraiture to an audience far greater than in earlier centuries and narrowed the gap between the idealized representation of a public figure and the penetrating depiction of a human being. The camera was perceived as a magical tool for capturing an image of exceptional fidelity, power, and brilliance. Even the absence of color and the small scale of the photograph were not seen as flaws in the new process; instead, they enhanced the special qualities of the new medium. Here was nature, reduced and frozen in time. At first the photograph was too slow for satisfactory portraiture, but stubborn experimentors quickly found a way to make exposures short enough to record the image of a living subject. The results were amazing to the public, and by the early 1840s portrait photographers had sprung up everywhere. By the middle of the nineteenth century professional portrait photographers had recognized the power of the portrait in series.

While these photographers did not assume the high moral tone of their predecessors, they evidently felt there was a substantial market for portraits of national leaders. Mathew Brady in America, Nadar in France, and scores of their contemporaries were determined to record the worthy faces of their time and make them available to the public. Legislators, war heroes, intellectual leaders, artists: all were eagerly sought by photographers wishing to record the appearance of those persons who shaped their civilization. The images at their best were compelling. Looking back at them today, we see in these direct photographs a record of the experience, temperament, and intellectual capacities of persons whose achievements we have come to respect, and whose names are household words.

Unlike the Roman portraits, these portraits are not idealized into a single mold, with comparatively slight allowances made for variations in physiognomy; nor was portraiture reserved for the mighty. Increasingly, the photographic portrait became attractive to the ordinary person. In the hands of talented photographers like Brady or Southworth and Hawes, the professional photographic portrait of the mid-nineteenth century burns with individuality.

As the nineteenth century progressed toward the twentieth vanity overtook the portrait. With the tendency toward pictorialism that made every photograph into an imitation painting or etching came the portrait photograph with as much retouching as photograph, in which features are regularized, blemishes removed, and the traces of age softened. The studio portrait flattered rather than recorded and as a result became empty of character.

Early in the twentieth century a few photographers became disenchanted with the vacant slickness of professional portrait photography and sought a "new objectivity" in their work, wishing to emphasize the clarity and range of tonal rendition they saw as the essential quality of the photograph. One of the most significant of these objective photographers was Germany's August Sander.

Sander was determined to record the ordinary people of his time—the butcher, the street cleaner, the civil servant, the maid—in a series of photographic portraits. In the end, these came to rival the earlier series that were devoted to sitters of prominence. The photographs are remarkable for their clarity and simplicity. While each person is depicted in a setting related to his profession, the settings are clearly subordinated. The subjects regard the camera (and, therefore, the viewer) with direct gazes, aware of the presence of the photographer but seemingly unaffected by it. None of Sander's subjects seems to be putting on a special face for the occasion or altering his personality in order to pretend to be something or someone he is not.

Michael Evans has carried the objectivity of Sander one step farther: his people are presented in an entirely neutral environment, and only a few are identified through the presence of some object used in everyday life. This use of a neutral background is not Evans's invention. Such noted photographers as Richard Avedon and Irving Penn have used the device to great effect. Avedon uses the empty background to isolate the closely studied faces of his subjects until the viewer becomes almost obsessively aware of the imperfections of the human form and the marks of age and care on those popularly regarded as ageless and carefree. In Penn's work the background becomes a device to obliterate cultural and economic lines; the clothing, pose, and countenance of his subject tell the whole story.

Evans has given uniformity to his series of portraits by selecting a single viewpoint and a similar pose for each of his subjects. These common elements are the framework for an amazing diversity; the individuality of each person Evans has photographed emerges with exceptional directness in this series. No two of his subjects stand in just the same way, face the lens exactly in the same way, or hold their hands identically.

Here, in the "objective" style of the twentieth century, are portraits of people about whom we are anything but objective. There is an aura of glamor about people in positions of power and about those who work close to those in power. We may differ politically with a prominent politician but he still has the capacity to attract our attention in a strange and gripping way. Curiously, men and women in public life are sometimes so overexposed that we cease really to see them, so it comes as a revelation in these portraits that these people have recaptured their individual personalities and ceased to be merely "public figures."

It is a curious fact that it has become unfashionable to care about creating a serious portrait record of those who make our laws, administer our government departments, and shape public opinion. Perhaps in this cynical age, when we rarely evoke the optimism and sense of moral mission held by Peale and Longacre and Herring, we have forgotten that we still want to know about those who are at the center of our government. Of course there are formal portraits of the Presidents and their cabinets of the past several decades, and the presidential libraries contain files of informal photographs of some of the people surrounding the chief executive, but until Michael Evans undertook this portrait project no one in recent years had attempted to bring together in a series of uniformly conceived photographs the people who are central to our government.

These portraits are neither idealized nor glamorized. They are essentially human documents of the people you would have seen in Washington during the years of the presidency of Ronald Reagan, depicted by a photographer who was often at the side of the President and was therefore in a position to judge who among the many legislators, journalists, government officials, and politicians impressed upon the consciousness of the chief executive. They are neutral in a partisan sense; the whole political spectrum is included, and the members of one party do not come off better than another. Evans has not done this as a celebration of political or moral virtue or as a model for future generations, except in one regard: we should be making a record of this kind for each administration.

In our age there is no longer much concern with recording and celebrating only the heroes of the republic. The richness and value of Evans's collection of portraits is that he has not limited himself to heroes. There is too little consensus about heroes, and, in any case, even life at the center of Washington involves many who are engaged in comparatively unheroic ventures. In Evans's view, these are the people who, for better or worse, make the republic work, and he has recognized that we ought to take account of them while they are gathered in their common purpose in our capital city. This is what Michael Evans has added to the historical record with such distinction, using the tools of photography with exceptional subtlety and judgment. His achievement must be a model for future chroniclers of the American presidency.

ALAN FERN

"We photographers deal in things which are continually vanishing."

—HENRI CARTIER-BRESSON

24

*"The contemplation of things as they are, without substitution
or imposture, without error and confusion, is in itself a nobler thing
than a whole harvest of invention."*

—SIR FRANCIS BACON
as quoted by Dorothea Lange

BARRY MORRIS GOLDWATER (R—ARIZONA)
United States Senator

26

JAMES SCOTT BRADY
Assistant to the President and Press Secretary

BENJAMIN CROWNINSHIELDS BRADLEE
Executive Editor, *The Washington Post*

ARTHUR FRANK BURNS
United States Ambassador to West Germany

29

ALLAN EZRA GOTLIEB
Ambassador to the United States from Canada

30

KATHARINE GRAHAM
Chairman of the Board, The Washington Post Company

CLARENCE McLANE PENDLETON, JR.
Chairman, United States Commission on Civil Rights

CASPAR WILLARD WEINBERGER
Secretary of Defense

HOWARD HENRY BAKER, JR. (R—TENNESSEE)
Majority Leader, United States Senate

THOMAS PHILIP (TIP) O'NEILL, JR. (D—MASSACHUSETTS)
Speaker, United States House of Representatives

WARREN EARL BURGER
Chief Justice, United States Supreme Court

STROM THURMOND (R—SOUTH CAROLINA)
President Pro Tempore, United States Senate

RONALD WILSON REAGAN
President of the United States

GEORGE PRATT SHULTZ
Secretary of State

GEORGE HERBERT WALKER BUSH
Vice-President of the United States

40

EDWIN MEESE III
Counsellor to the President

BARBARA PIERCE BUSH
Wife of the Vice-President of the United States

41

RICHARD VINCENT ALLEN
Assistant to the President for National Security Affairs, 1981–82

SANDRA DAY O'CONNOR
United States Supreme Court Associate Justice

CHESTER TRENT LOTT (R—MISSISSIPPI)
United States Representative

FRED FISHER FIELDING
Counsel to the President

JACK SMITH
Vice-President and Washington Bureau Chief,
Columbia Broadcasting System

45

THE HONORABLE WILLIAM EDWARD SIMON
Chairman of the Board, Wesray Corporation

DANIEL AUGUST RUGE, M.D.
Personal Physician to the President

46

HENRY JOHN HYDE (R—ILLINOIS)
United States Representative

47

JOSEPH COORS
President, Adolph Coors Company

49

ROBERT JOSEPH DOLE (R—KANSAS)
United States Senator

WILLIAM PATRICK CLARK
Secretary of the Interior

MARY ELLEN (MEG) GREENFIELD
Editorial Page Editor, *The Washington Post*

52

ROBERT DAVID NOVAK
Syndicated Columnist

53

RICHARD BERNARD STONE
Presidential Special Envoy to Central America

RICHARD GORDON DARMAN
Assistant to the President and Deputy to the Chief of Staff

54

ROBERT HENRY MICHEL (R—ILLINOIS)
Republican Leader, United States House of Representatives

JOHN CORNELIUS STENNIS (D—MISSISSIPPI)
United States Senator

YOSHIO OKAWARA
Ambassador to the United States from Japan

JEANE JORDAN KIRKPATRICK
United States Representative to the United Nations

PETER McCOY
Assistant to the President and Chief of Staff
to the First Lady, 1981–82

JAMES SCOTT ROSEBUSH
Deputy Assistant to the President
and Chief of Staff to the First Lady

58

FRED JOSEPH MAROON
Freelance Photographer/Author

MARTIN PERETZ
Editor-in-Chief and President, *The New Republic*

JOHN CLAGGETT DANFORTH (R—MISSOURI)
United States Senator

MORTON MATT KONDRACKE
Executive Editor, *The New Republic*

PHILIP MERRILL
Publisher and President, *The Washingtonian*

61

JOSEPH KRAFT
Syndicated Columnist, *Los Angeles Times*

MICHAEL KEITH DEAVER
Assistant to the President and Deputy Chief of Staff

FRANKLYN CURRAN NOFZIGER
Senior Partner, Nofziger & Bragg

HARLON BRONSON CARTER
Executive Vice-President, National Rifle Association

LIEUTENANT COLONEL TERENCE DAKE
Commanding Officer, Marine Helicopter, Squadron One

COLONEL ROBERT EARL RUDDICK
Presidential Pilot

65

DAVID ALLEN STOCKMAN
Director, Office of Management and Budget

CLAUDE DENSON PEPPER (D—FLORIDA)
United States Representative

DAN DANIEL (D—VIRGINIA)
United States Representative

ROGER JASON STONE, JR.
Eastern Regional Campaign Director, Reagan-Bush Committee

JOSEPH WALTER CANZERI
Assistant to the President and Assistant
to the Deputy Chief of Staff, 1981–82

ARAM BAKSHIAN, JR.
Deputy Assistant to the President and Director
of the Presidential Speechwriting Office, 1981–83

MARGARET DEBARDELEBEN TUTWILER
Executive Assistant to the Chief of Staff,
The White House

HARVEY LEROY (LEE) ATWATER
Special Assistant to the President
for Political Affairs, 1981–83

LYNN MORLEY MARTIN (R—ILLINOIS)
United States Representative

GILLESPIE V. (SONNY) MONTGOMERY
(D—MISSISSIPPI)
United States Representative

DAVID HUME KENNERLY
Contract Photographer, *Time*

ROBERT CARL McFARLANE
Deputy Assistant to the President for National Security Affairs

74

PATRICK JOSEPH LEAHY (D—VERMONT)
United States Senator

ANDREW LINDSAY (DREW) LEWIS, JR.
Secretary of Transportation, 1981–83

SAM AUGUSTUS NUNN (D—GEORGIA)
United States Senator

JAMES ANDERSON BAKER III
Assistant to the President and Chief of Staff

78

WILLIAM FRENCH SMITH
Attorney General of the United States

MARVIN LAWRENCE STONE
Editor, *U.S. News & World Report*

JOHN CARTER BROWN
Director, National Gallery of Art, and Director, Commission on Fine Arts

80

SIDNEY DILLON RIPLEY, JR.
Secretary, Smithsonian Institution

DONALD THOMAS REGAN
Secretary of the Treasury

83

JEROME ROBERT ZIPKIN
Investor

WILLIAM JOSEPH CASEY
Director, Central Intelligence Agency

85

REVEREND TIMOTHY STAFFORD HEALY, S.J.
President, Georgetown University

86

RODDEY EARL MIMS
Contract Photographer, *Time*

A. C. LYLES
Motion Picture and Television Producer

MARK DAVID WEINBERG
Assistant Press Secretary to the President

LEE ADRIEN LESCAZE
New York News Editor, *The Wall Street Journal*

CLIFFORD EVANS
Vice-President, Washington Bureau,
RKO General Broadcasting

DEAN FRANCIS REYNOLDS
White House Correspondent, Cable News Network

WILLIAM ALBERT WILSON
United States Ambassador to the Holy See

ROBERT DANE McFARLAND
Vice-President and Washington Bureau Chief,
National Broadcasting Company

89

GEORGE TAMES
Chief Photographer, Washington Bureau, *The New York Times*

JOHN SCOTT APPLEWHITE
Staff Photographer, The Associated Press

MABEL HOBART (MUFFIE) BRANDON
Social Secretary, The White House, 1981–83

WALLACE WILLIAM McNAMEE
Staff Photographer, *Newsweek*

EFREM ZIMBALIST, JR.
Actor

STEVEN ROGER WEISMAN
White House Correspondent, *The New York Times*

DIRCK STORM HALSTEAD
Senior White House Photographer, *Time*

96

ROGER LACEY STEVENS
Chairman of the Board, The John F. Kennedy Center

CHARLES HARTING PERCY (R—ILLINOIS)
United States Senator

CHRISTOPHER WALLACE
White House Correspondent, National Broadcasting Company

EDWARD JOHN ROLLINS, JR.
Assistant to the President for Political Affairs, 1982–83

EDGAR THEODORE (TED) GRABER
Interior Designer for the White House

JOHN HOWARD NELSON
Washington Bureau Chief, *Los Angeles Times*

100

WILLIAM LEWIS SAFIRE
Columnist, *The New York Times*

PAUL ADOLPH VOLCKER
Chairman, Federal Reserve Board

102

SOL MYRON LINOWITZ
Senior Counsel, Coudert Brothers

THEODORE FULTON STEVENS (R—ALASKA)
United States Senator

JACK MOSELEY
Chairman, U.S. Fidelity & Guarantee Company

MEIR ROSENNE
Ambassador to the United States from Israel

103

104

GUY VANDER JAGT (R—MICHIGAN)
United States Representative

JAMES THOMAS BROYHILL (R—NORTH CAROLINA)
United States Representative

105

LIEUTENANT GENERAL JAMES ARTHUR WILLIAMS
Director, Defense Intelligence Agency

BRENT SCOWCROFT
Chairman, President's Commission on Strategic Forces

BENTLY THOMAS ELLIOTT
Deputy Assistant to the President
and Director of Speechwriting

ADMIRAL BOBBY RAY INMAN (RETIRED)
Director, National Security Agency, 1977–81

ANDREA MITCHELL
White House Correspondent,
National Broadcasting Company

JUDY WOODRUFF
Chief Washington Correspondent,
McNeil-Lehrer News Hour

DIANA DICKEN McLELLAN
Syndicated Columnist

ELEANOR IRENE ROELOFFS CLIFT
White House Correspondent, *Newsweek*

ALEXANDER MORGAN MASON
Special Assistant to the President, 1981–83

109

LARRY MELVIN SPEAKES
Assistant to the President and Principal Deputy Press Secretary

CHARLES Z. WICK
Director, United States Information Agency

HENRY MARTIN (SCOOP) JACKSON (D—WASHINGTON)
United States Senator

DAVID CHARLES FISCHER
Personal Aide to the President

ROBERT MARK WARNER
Archivist of the United States

112

EDWIN LELAND HARPER
Deputy Assistant to the President for Policy Development

RICHARD BITNER WIRTHLIN
Presidential Pollster and President,
Decision-Making Information

113

CRAIG LAWRENCE FULLER
Assistant to the President for Cabinet Affairs

JOHN JOSEPH McLAUGHLIN
Washington Executive Editor, *National Review*,
and Producer & Moderator, The McLaughlin Group

J. LYNN HELMS
Administrator, Federal Aviation Administration

EDWARD VINCENT HICKEY, JR.
Assistant to the President and Director
of Special Support Services

115

116

BRUCE KERRY CHAPMAN
Deputy Assistant to the President and Director,
Planning and Evaluation

MELVILLE PETER McPHERSON
Administrator, Agency for International Development

117

BRUCE KING MacLAURY
President, The Brookings Institution

HUGH SWANSON SIDEY
Washington Contributing Editor, *Time*

ELISABETH BUMILLER
Reporter, *The Washington Post*

MARK ODOM HATFIELD, JR.
Staff Assistant to the President, Office of Presidential Advance

WILLIAM HEDGECOCK WEBSTER
Director, Federal Bureau of Investigation

122

RAYMOND JAMES DONOVAN
Secretary of Labor

EARLE MOGAN JORGENSEN
Chairman of the Board and Chief Executive Officer, The Earle M. Jorgensen Company

124

BOB JOHN ROBISON
Managing Director and Executive Vice-President, Hill & Knowlton, Inc.

HOLLAND HANSON COORS
Director, Citizens for a New Beginning

CHARLES EVERETT KOOP, M.D.
Surgeon General of the United States

DANIEL ROSTENKOWSKI (D—ILLINOIS)
United States Representative

128

HOLMES PAUL TUTTLE
Retired President and Chairman of the Board, Holmes Tuttle, Inc.

BILL KOVACH
Washington Editor, *The New York Times*

GENERAL JOHN WILLIAM VESSEY, JR.
Chairman, Joint Chiefs of Staff

GENERAL CHARLES ALVIN GABRIEL
Chief of Staff, United States Air Force

GENERAL JOHN ADAMS WICKHAM, JR.
Chief of Staff, United States Army

ADMIRAL JAMES DAVID WATKINS
Chief of Naval Operations

GENERAL PAUL XAVIER KELLEY
Commandant, United States Marine Corps

LOU CANNON
White House Correspondent, *The Washington Post*

133

ROBERT KEITH GRAY
Chairman, Gray & Company

EDGAR PENDLETON JAMES
Assistant to the President for Presidential Personnel, 1981–82

STANLEY TRETICK
Staff Photographer, *People*

NANCY J. RISQUE
Special Assistant to the President and Deputy Director,
Office of Legislative Affairs

SIR OLIVER WRIGHT
Her Britannic Majesty's Ambassador to the United States

138

MARK ODOM HATFIELD, SR. (R—OREGON)
United States Senator

ROSCOE LYNN EGGER, JR.
Commissioner, Internal Revenue Service

MAJOR PETER TODD METZGER
Marine Aide to the President

COMMANDER WILLIAM GLENN SUTTON
Naval Aide to the President

MAJOR WILLIAM M. DRENNAN, JR.
Air Force Aide to the President

MAJOR CHARLES FORD BROWER IV
Army Aide to the President

WILLIAM FREDERICK BOLGER
Postmaster General

DANIEL JOSEPH BOORSTIN
The Librarian of Congress

M. B. OGLESBY, JR.
Assistant to the President for Congressional Affairs

KENNETH WILLARD DAM
Deputy Secretary of State

143

144

LOWELL PALMER WEICKER, JR. (R—CONNECTICUT)
United States Senator

145

JOHN RUSLING BLOCK
Secretary of Agriculture

JAMES GAIUS WATT
Secretary of the Interior, 1981–83

147

ARLEN SPECTER (R—PENNSYLVANIA)
United States Senator

MARTIN CARL ANDERSON
Assistant to the President for Policy Development,
1981–82

SARAH NEWCOMB McCLENDON
White House Correspondent, McClendon News Service

WALTER HUBERT ANNENBERG
President, Triangle Publications

WILLIAM PLANTE
White House Correspondent,
Columbia Broadcasting System

KATHLEEN OSBORNE
Personal Secretary to the President

150

MASTER SERGEANT CORNELL JENNINGS
Transportation Supervisor, The White House

ROBERT LEE DePROSPERO
Special Agent in Charge of the Presidential Protective
Division, United States Secret Service

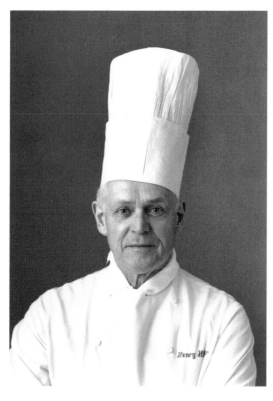

HENRY HALLER
Executive Chef, The White House

MILTON HOMER PITTS
Presidential Hair Stylist

151

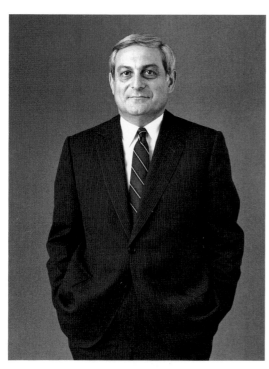

SET CHARLES MOMJIAN
Member of the
United States Holocaust Commission

CAROLYNE KAHLE DAVIS
Administrator,
Health Care Financing Administration

JEREMIA ALOYSIUS O'LEARY, JR.
White House Correspondent, *The Washington Times*

ROWLAND EVANS
Syndicated Columnist

153

WILLIAM JOHN BENNETT
Chairman, National Endowment for the Humanities

154

ANGELA MARIE BUCHANAN
United States Treasurer, 1981–83

FRANK BERNARD JOHNSTON
Staff Photographer, *The Washington Post*

BECKY NORTON DUNLOP
Deputy Assistant to the President
for Presidential Personnel

CHARLES PARRY TYSON
Deputy Assistant to the President for
National Security Affairs

FREDERICK JOSEPH RYAN, JR.
Special Assistant and Director of Appointments
and Scheduling to the President

GAHL LEE HODGES
Social Secretary, The White House

156

JOHN FRANCIS WILLIAM ROGERS
Assistant to the President for Management

DONALD PAUL HODEL
Secretary of Energy

157

JOSEPH VERNER REED, JR.
Ambassador of the United States to the Kingdom of Morocco

WILLIAM VON RAAB
Commissioner, United States Customs Service

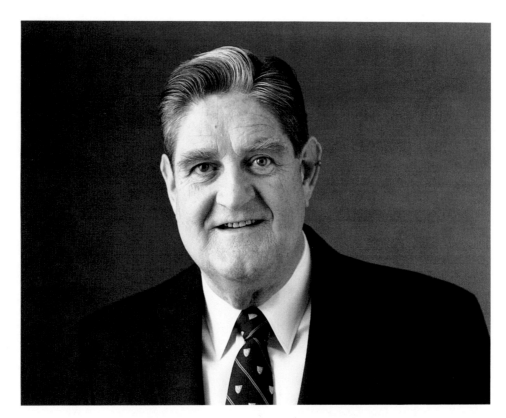

HOWELL THOMAS HEFLIN (D—ALABAMA)
United States Senator

158

GEORGE (RAY) CULLIN, JR.
White House Field Producer, National Broadcasting Company

159

PAUL DOMINIQUE LAXALT (R—NEVADA)
United States Senator

JOHN GOODWIN TOWER (R—TEXAS)
United States Senator

PAULA FICKES HAWKINS (R—FLORIDA)
United States Senator

GEORGE ALBERT KEYWORTH II
Science Advisor to the President

WILLIAM SEBASTIAN COHEN (R—MAINE)
United States Senator

163

RICHARD VIGURIE
President, The Vigurie Company

FAITH RYAN WHITTLESEY
Assistant to the President for Public Liaison

ALAN GREEN, JR.
Chairman, Federal Maritime Commission

PATRICK JOSEPH BUCHANAN
Syndicated Columnist

165

LAWRENCE SIDNEY EAGLEBURGER
Under Secretary for Political Affairs, Department of State,
1982–84

167

HENRY BRANDON
Fellow, Brookings Institution

KENNETH LEE ADELMAN
Director, Arms Control and Disarmament Agency

168

JACK FRENCH KEMP (R—NEW YORK)
United States Representative

169

JAMES JARRELL PICKLE (D—TEXAS)
United States Representative

RICHARD BRUCE CHENEY (R—WYOMING)
United States Representative

ADMIRAL JAMES STEELE GRACEY
Commandant, United States Coast Guard

REAR ADMIRAL JOHN MARLAN POINDEXTER
Deputy Assistant to the President for
National Security Affairs

171

LAURENCE IRWIN BARRETT
Senior White House Correspondent, *Time*

EDWARD MICHAEL FOUHY
Vice-President and Washington Bureau Chief, ABC News

172

WILLIAM FREDERICK SITTMAN
Special Assistant to the President
and Special Assistant to the Deputy Chief of Staff

PETER BARTON WILSON (R—CALIFORNIA)
United States Senator

173

HENRY JOHN HEINZ III (R—PENNSYLVANIA)
United States Senator

DAVID RICHMOND GERGEN
Assistant to the President for Communications, 1981–84

175

SAMUEL RILEY PIERCE, JR.
Secretary of Housing and Urban Development

176

JAMES MONTGOMERY BEGGS
Administrator, National Aeronautics and
Space Administration

GERALD POSNER CARMEN
Administrator, General Services Administration

CLEMENT ELLIS CONGER
Curator, The White House

DONALD HENRY RUMSFELD
Special Envoy to the Middle East, 1983–84

177

178

NEWTON LEROY GINGRICH (R—GEORGIA)
United States Representative

ADMIRAL DANIEL JOSEPH MURPHY
Chief of Staff to the Vice-President

179

MARTIN STUART FELDSTEIN
Chairman, Council of Economic Advisors

LOYE WHEAT MILLER, JR.
White House Correspondent, Newhouse Newspapers

ROGER BLAINE PORTER
Deputy Assistant to the President and Director of Policy Development

181

HENRY SALVATORI
Founder and Retired President and Chairman of the Board, Western Geophysical Company

182

WILLIAM PHILIP (PHIL) GRAMM (R—TEXAS)
United States Representative

ALEXANDER MEIGS HAIG, JR.
Secretary of State, 1981–82

GARY FRANCIS SCHUSTER
Washington Bureau Chief, *The Detroit News*

WILLIAM EMERSON BROCK
United States Trade Representative

FRANK JOSEPH FAHRENKOPF, JR.
Chairman, Republican National Committee

186

MICHAEL CHARLES CURB
Chairman, Republican National Finance Committee

MARK RUSSELL
Political Comedian

JOHN ALFRED SVAHN
Assistant to the President for Policy Development

JAMES CLIFFORD MILLER III
Chairman, Federal Trade Commission

JOHN FRANCIS LEHMAN, JR.
Secretary of the Navy

VERNE ORR
Secretary of the Air Force

189

HERBERT EUGENE ELLINGWOOD
Chairman, Merit Systems Protection Board

PETER DOR HANNAFORD
Chairman of the Board and Chief Executive Officer,
The Hannaford Company, Inc.

190

AUSTIN HUNTINGTON KIPLINGER
President, The Kiplinger Washington Editors, Inc.

RALPH ROBERT LINOWES
Senior Partner, Linowes & Blocher

RICHARD SCHULTZ SCHWEIKER
Secretary of Health and Human Services, 1981–83

192

PATRICK BRUCE OLIPHANT
Syndicated Editorial Cartoonist

ARTHUR LEVITT, JR.
Chairman, American Stock Exchange

CHARLES EUGENE (PAT) BOONE
Entertainer

WILLIAM DOYLE RUCKELSHAUS
Administrator, Environmental Protection Agency

MEL ELFIN
Washington Bureau Chief, *Newsweek*

LEE LOVELY VERSTANDIG
Assistant to the President for Intergovernmental Affairs

DIANA HARDIN WALKER
Contract Photographer, *Time*

LAWRENCE STEVEN DOWNING
Staff Photographer, *Newsweek*

196

YOICHI ROBERT OKAMOTO
Freelance Photographer

FREDERICK WARD
Staff Photographer, Black Star Agency

JAMES CLAUDE WRIGHT, JR. (D—TEXAS)
United States Representative

198

MALCOLM BALDRIGE
Secretary of Commerce

199

BARBER BENJAMIN CONABLE, JR. (R—NEW YORK)
United States Representative

WILLIAM VICTOR ROTH, JR. (R—DELAWARE)
United States Senator

ROBERT WILLIAM PACKWOOD (R—OREGON)
United States Senator

CHARLES McCURDY MATHIAS, JR. (R—MARYLAND)
United States Senator

202

JUSTIN WHITLOCK DART
Chairman of the Executive Committee, Dart & Kraft, Inc.

203

PAUL HENRY NITZE
Special Representative for the United States Arms Control and Disarmament Agency

HELEN AMELIA THOMAS
White House Bureau Chief, United Press International

MAUREEN ELIZABETH REAGAN
Daughter of the President of the United States
and Special Consultant to the
Republican National Committee

ANN WOODRUFF COMPTON
White House Correspondent,
American Broadcasting Company

REX WAYNE SCOUTEN
Chief Usher, The White House

DONNA KOLNIK POPE
Director, The United States Mint

ALAN CURTIS NELSON
Commissioner,
Immigration and Naturalization Service

206

JOHN STEWART HERRINGTON
Assistant to the President
for Presidential Personnel

SILVIO OTTAVIO CONTE (R—MASSACHUSETTS)
United States Representative

KATHERINE DAVALOS ORTEGA
Treasurer of the United States

LESLEY STAHL
White House Correspondent, Columbia Broadcasting System

209

MAX LEE FRIEDERSDORF
Assistant to the President for Congressional Affairs, 1981–82

KENNETH MARC DUBERSTEIN
Assistant to the President for Legislative Affairs, 1982–83

MARION BARRY, JR.
Mayor of Washington, District of Columbia

COLONEL MATTHEW PATRICK CAULFIELD
Deputy Director, Military Office, The White House

SELWA SHOWKER ROOSEVELT
Chief of Protocol of the United States

CHARLES HARDING VIOLETTE
Technician, Columbia Broadcasting System

CAL ASHBY MARLIN
Staff Cameraman, Columbia Broadcasting System

LARRY ALAN RUBINSTEIN
Staff Photographer, United Press International

HOWELL HIRAM RAINES
National Political Correspondent,
The New York Times

WALTER BIGELOW WRISTON
Chairman of the Board,
Citibank National Association

214

PETER HERMES
Ambassador to the United States from the
Federal Republic of Germany

MORRIS DRAPER
Ambassador and Special Presidential Emissary
to the Middle East

DANIEL JAMES TERRA
Ambassador at Large for Cultural Affairs

STUART KRIEG SPENCER
President, Spencer-Roberts & Associates

BERYL WAYNE SPRINKEL
Under Secretary, Department of the Treasury

KEN CURTIS
Actor

ANNE VOLZ HIGGINS
Special Assistant to the President and
Director of Correspondence

EDDIE SERANO
Assistant Food Service Coordinator, The White House

JENNINGS RANDOLPH (D—WEST VIRGINIA)
United States Senator

MAUREEN LOUISE SANTINI
Senior White House Correspondent, The Associated Press

220

PATRICIA SUE JACOBSON
Texas Republican Executive Committeewoman

GOLDIE LEONORE ARTHUR
Volunteer for Reagan-Bush Celebrity Committee

BERNIE BOSTON
Staff Photographer, *Los Angeles Times*

221

222

MICHAEL ARTHUR WORDEN EVANS
Personal Photographer to the President and President, The Portrait Project, Inc.

AFTERWORD

In November of 1981 I approached Michael K. Deaver, Assistant to the President and Deputy Chief of Staff, with the idea of putting together a matched set of photographic portraits of people whom *The New York Times* would later call "the Movers and Shakers of Washington." This collection would supplement my pictorial coverage at the White House, and would be another way of documenting the Reagan presidency. Deaver enthusiastically endorsed the project, but warned me of the difficulties of persuading busy people to add portrait sittings to their schedules.

I set to work drawing up a nonpartisan list of people in government, the media, and private life whose activities have (or have had) an effect on this administration, or who were influential in the President's early political career. I also added to this list a number of career government employees whose work supports the President.

The list soon numbered just over 700 names, and every morning a casual reading of the newspapers would remind me of someone I had forgotten.

My next step was to organize a test photography session to refine my concept with a physical result. Looking for suitable "studio" space for a test, I mentioned my problem to Story Shem, who, along with Marthena Cowart and Iris Jacobson, runs the Washington-based logistics and public relations company called Arrive Unlimited.

Difficult though the problem of housing the test seemed to be, it was trivial to the worthy operatives of Arrive. One Saturday in early December 1981 we simply dismantled Arrive's office in a townhouse on Q Street in downtown Washington. Having invited fifty people for the next day, I proceeded to photograph them at ten-minute intervals. We provided wine and snacks, and by ten-thirty that night I was cross-eyed from staring into the viewfinder.

Despite its rigors the test session produced a number of portraits that pleased me as well as my subjects. Coincidentally I also fell in love with Story Shem—who is even more beautiful than she is organized—and married her two years later.

The test session proved that my dream could be realized, and so I set up a more or less permanent studio in a Washington brownstone. It was there that I

223

made the bulk of the photographs that came to be called The Portrait Project. In addition, I had one session in Los Angeles portraying some of the President's California associates and several sessions in a temporary studio I set up on Capitol Hill.

Acquiring subjects proved not as easy as I first assumed. During the course of my photographic activities at the White House I would ambush Cabinet officers and other government officials before meetings or other events. At Washington gatherings of all kinds I would scan the room with eagle eye and pounce on people avidly. Meeting people face to face was very effective in convincing them to "sit" for me. But I also spent long hours at my trusty Apple II+ computer writing letters to entice potential victims. In this I had a clear precedent in Mathew Brady, the noted Civil War–era photographer who maintained studios in Washington and New York and photographed just about everybody of importance in his time. Brady also engaged in an active letter-lobbying campaign. A letter of his to Vice-President–elect Andrew Johnson survives in the Library of Congress. In it, on May 2, 1865, he wrote:

Dear Sir,

I have repeated calls every hour in the day for your photograph and would regard it as a great favor if you could give me a sitting to day so that I may be able to exhibit a large picture on the 4th. If you cannot call today please call at your earliest convenience and very much oblig.

Yours truly,
M. B. Brady

Some 120 years later, I can sympathize fully!

Of course Brady lived in much simpler times when the ordinary citizen could and did stroll up to the front portico of the White House at almost any time of day and knock on the door. It was not unheard of for the President to receive such unscheduled visitors.

Those who agreed to pose for Brady, however, had to be prepared for some arduous doings. A photograph made by Brady involved an exposure of anywhere from thirty seconds during the bright light of summer to six minutes in the dim of winter. The sitter's head would be firmly clamped in a heavy, viselike metal apparatus planted solidly on the floor of the studio behind the subject, hidden from the camera. (No wonder some of Brady's portraits have been described as riveting!) The sessions sometimes lasted for hours, for the "film" that Brady used consisted of glass "wet plates," which had to remain wet during the exposure and then be rushed into the darkroom for development.

Though modern technology has made my photographic process much quicker and easier, my self-imposed challenge added to my basic responsibility to the President has made the last fifteen months into something of a blur. Portraits, Presidential trips to California, Hawaii, Guam, Japan, Korea, China, Ireland, England, France—and more portraits. But I remember with particular fondness three incidents.

One of my subjects did not care for my first attempt to portray him. A second sitting was arranged. By mistake I re-sent the original portrait. On receipt of the "new" portrait the subject called me personally with congratulations on the improvement in the new version!

One senator's appointments secretary turned me down, saying, "The senator never goes to that part of town." What he had against the eminently respectable Dupont Circle area of Washington I never did find out, but eventually he sat for his protrait.

Then there was the time I mentioned the name of the late photographer and ardent conservationist Ansel Adams to James Watt, then Secretary of the Interior and much under attack by environmentalists. It only took me ten minutes to calm him down!

Not surprisingly, in an enterprise of this scope I have been aided and assisted by many people. I thank them all, but in particular I would like to recognize and thank the following:

Yoichi Okamoto, David Hume Kennerly, Dirck Halstead, Irving Penn, Richard Avedon, Yousuf Karsh, Erich Salomon, and August Sander, who came before, and whose work is a constant source of wonder and inspiration;

Arnold Drapkin, John Durniak, and John G. Morris, picture editors and my mentors, who led me to find in myself what they saw in me;

Alan Fern of the National Portrait Gallery and Jane Livingston of the Corcoran Gallery of Art for their faith and constructive criticism;

Set Momjian, David Shakarian, and Richard Manoogian; Peter Diamandis of CBS Magazine Division; and Susan S. Bloom, The American Express Company, for generous financial support of the Project's activities;

George Hiotis, my companion on the road over many political miles and a friend, whose technical abilities as my photographic assistant over the last four years contributed greatly to the "look" of these portraits;

Howard Berg and Don Penny, who believed in the Project right from the start;

Chuck Trainum, the Portrait Project's counsel;

Senators Howard Baker and Patrick Leahy and Jo Tartt for their interest and service on the board of the Portrait Project;

Louise Bell, my faithful and tireless assistant;

Billie Shaddix, my administrative aide at the White House, and his assistant, Jayn Monteith;

Carol Greenawalt, the White House picture editor, and her assistant, Diane Powers, who have put up with me patiently for the last four years;

Bill Fitz-Patrick, Pete Souza, Jack Kightlinger, and Mary Ann Fackelman, official White House photographers of talent and devotion, who have shared with me a great adventure and whose images enrich the historical record;

David C. Fischer, the President's personal aide, who has shared many long hours on the road and has never lost his sense of humor;

Ken Duberstein and Nancy Risque, who helped me navigate the corridors of Capitol Hill;

Lyn Nofziger and Morgan Mason for wise counsel;

Phil Merrill, John Sansing, Jack Limpert, and Linda Otto of *The Washingtonian*;

Carla Peterson, my indefatigable researcher;

Paul Gottlieb, Bob Morton, Shun Yamamoto, Sam Antupit, Judith Michael, and Beverly Fazio of Harry Abrams, who have proved with this book that speed and quality can be compatible;

Barbara Strauss-Locke of Osawa, Inc., and the Eastman Kodak Company for valuable technical assistance;

Jason Horowitz, a gifted printer and photographer, who got everything there was to get from my negatives for this book.

Finally, to my patient subjects, who may not have always known exactly why they were posing but who took me on faith: The Portrait Project is a tribute to you.

MICHAEL EVANS

INDEX OF NAMES

In addition to the name of the subject and the number of the page on which his or her photograph appears, the index also provides the subject's date and place of birth.

Joseph Coors, 48
November 12, 1917
Denver, Colorado

George (Ray) Cullin, Jr., 158
August 30, 1931
Amarillo, Texas

Michael Charles Curb, 186
December 24, 1944
Savannah, Georgia

Ken Curtis, 217
July 2, 1916
Lamar, Colorado

Lieutenant Colonel Terence Dake, 65
July 22, 1944
Omaha, Nebraska

Kenneth Willard Dam, 143
August 10, 1932
Marysville, Kansas

John Claggett Danforth, 59
September 5, 1936
Saint Louis, Missouri

Dan Daniel, 68
May 12, 1914
Chatham, Virginia

Richard Gordon Darman, 53
May 10, 1943
Charlotte, North Carolina

Justin Whitlock Dart, 202
August 17, 1907
Evanston, Illinois
Died 1984

Carolyne Kahle Davis, 151
January 31, 1932
Penn Yan, New York

Michael Keith Deaver, 62
April 11, 1938
Bakersfield, California

Robert Lee DeProspero, 150
December 31, 1938
Morgantown, West Virginia

Robert Joseph Dole, 49
July 22, 1923
Russell, Kansas

Raymond James Donovan, 122
August 31, 1930
Bayonne, New Jersey

Lawrence Steven Downing, 196
November 12, 1952
San Fernando, California

Morris Draper, 214
February 18, 1928
Berkeley, California

Major William M. Drennan, Jr., 140
January 28, 1945
Greenville, South Carolina

Kenneth Marc Duberstein, 209
April 21, 1944
Brooklyn, New York

Becky Norton Dunlop, 155
October, 2, 1951
Minneapolis, Minnesota

Lawrence Sidney Eagleburger, 166
August 1, 1930
Milwaukee, Wisconsin

Roscoe Lynn Egger, Jr., 139
September 19, 1920
Jackson, Michigan

Mel Elfin, 195
July 18, 1929
Brooklyn, New York

Herbert Eugene Ellingwood, 190
March 5, 1931
Ordway, Colorado

Bently Thomas Elliott, 106
November 6, 1944
Bryn Mawr, Pennsylvania

Clifford Evans, 88
March 21, 1915
Brooklyn, New York
Died 1983

Michael Arthur Worden Evans, 222
June 24, 1944
Saint Louis, Missouri

Rowland Evans, 152
April 28, 1921
White Marsh, Pennsylvania

Frank Joseph Fahrenkopf, Jr., 186
August 28, 1939
Brooklyn, New York

Martin Stuart Feldstein, 179
November 25, 1939
New York, New York

Alan Fern, 18
October 19, 1930
Detroit, Michigan

Fred Fisher Fielding, 45
March 21, 1939
Philadelphia, Pennsylvania

David Charles Fischer, 112
January 21, 1948
Sandusky, Ohio

Edward Michael Fouhy, 171
November 30, 1934
Boston, Massachusetts

Max Lee Friedersdorf, 209
July 7, 1929
Grammer, Indiana

Craig Lawrence Fuller, 114
February 16, 1951
Pasadena, California

General Charles Alvin Gabriel, 131
January 21, 1928
Lincolnton, North Carolina

David Richmond Gergen, 174
May 9, 1942
Durham, North Carolina

Newton Leroy Gingrich, 178
June 17, 1943
Harrisburg, Pennsylvania

Barry Morris Goldwater, 25
January 1, 1909
Phoenix, Territory of Arizona

Allan Ezra Gotlieb, 29
February 28, 1928
Winnipeg, Canada

Edgar Theodore (Ted) Graber, 99
July 1, 1919
Los Angeles, California

Admiral James Steele Gracey, 170
August 24, 1927
Newton, Massachusetts

Katharine Graham, 30
June 16, 1917
New York, New York

William Philip (Phil) Gramm, 182
July 8, 1942
Fort Benning, Georgia

Robert Keith Gray, 133
September 2, 1921
Hastings, Nebraska

Alan Green, Jr., 165
May 1, 1925
Portland, Oregon

Mary Ellen (Meg) Greenfield, 51
December 27, 1930
Seattle, Washington

Alexander Meigs Haig, Jr., 183
December 2, 1924
Philadelphia, Pennsylvania

Henry Haller, 151
January 10, 1923
Altdorf, Switzerland

Dirck Storm Halstead, 95
December 24, 1936
Huntington, New York

Peter Dor Hannaford, 190
September 21, 1932
Glendale, California

Edwin Leland Harper, 113
November 13, 1941
Belleville, Illinois

Mark Odom Hatfield, Jr., 120
June 19, 1960
Salem, Oregon

Mark Odom Hatfield, Sr., 138
July 12, 1922
Dallas, Oregon

Paula Fickes Hawkins, 161
January 24, 1927
Salt Lake City, Utah

Reverend Timothy Stafford Healy, S.J., 85
April 25, 1923
New York, New York

Howell Thomas Heflin, 158
June 19, 1921
Poulan, Georgia

Henry John Heinz III, 173
October 23, 1938
Pittsburgh, Pennsylvania

J. Lynn Helms, 115
March 11, 1925
DeQueen, Arkansas

Peter Hermes, 214
August 8, 1922
Berlin, West Germany

John Stewart Herrington, 206
May 31, 1939
Los Angeles, California

Edward Vincent Hickey, Jr., 115
July 15, 1935
Dedham, Massachusetts

Anne Volz Higgins, 217
October 7, 1939
Bronx, New York

Donald Paul Hodel, 156
May 23, 1935
Portland, Oregon

Gahl Lee Hodges, 155
May 29, 1953
Washington, District of Columbia

Henry John Hyde, 47
April 8, 1924
Chicago, Illinois

Admiral Bobby Ray Inman, 106
April 4, 1931
Rhonesboro, Texas

Henry Martin (Scoop) Jackson, 111
May 31, 1912
Everett, Washington
Died 1983

Patricia Sue Jacobson, 220
December 23, 1926
Houston, Texas

Edgar Pendleton James, 134
October 23, 1929
Fort Smith, Arkansas

Master Sergeant Cornell Jennings, 150
May 29, 1947
Tiptonville, Tennessee

Frank Bernard Johnston, 154
May 25, 1941
Philadelphia, Pennsylvania

Earle Mogan Jorgensen, 123
June 22, 1898
San Francisco, California

General Paul Xavier Kelley, 131
November 11, 1928
Boston, Massachusetts

Jack French Kemp, 168
July 13, 1935
Los Angeles, California

David Hume Kennerly, 72
March 9, 1947
Roseburg, Oregon

George Albert Keyworth II, 162
November 30, 1939
Boston, Massachusetts

Austin Huntington Kiplinger, 190
September 19, 1918
Washington, District of Columbia

Jeane Jordan Kirkpatrick, 57
November 19, 1926
Duncan, Oklahoma

Morton Matt Kondracke, 60
April 28, 1939
Chicago, Illinois

Charles Everett Koop, 126
October 14, 1916
Brooklyn, New York

Bill Kovach, 129
September 16, 1932
Greenville, Tennessee

Joseph Kraft, 61
September 4, 1924
South Orange, New Jersey

Paul Dominique Laxalt, 159
August 2, 1922
Reno, Nevada

Patrick Joseph Leahy, 74
March 31, 1940
Montpelier, Vermont

John Francis Lehman, Jr., 189
September 14, 1942
Philadelphia, Pennsylvania

Lee Adrien Lescaze, 87
December 8, 1983
New York, New York

Arthur Levitt, Jr., 192
February 3, 1938
Brooklyn, New York

Andrew Lindsay (Drew) Lewis, Jr., 75
November 3, 1931
Philadelphia, Pennsylvania

Ralph Robert Linowes, 190
February 15, 1922
Trenton, New Jersey

Sol Myron Linowitz, 102
December 7, 1913
Trenton, New Jersey

Jane S. Livingston, 12
February 12, 1944
Upland, California

Chester Trent Lott, 44
October 9, 1941
Grenada, Mississippi

A. C. Lyles, 86
May 17, 1918
Jacksonville, Florida

Bruce King MacLaury, 117
May 7, 1931
Mount Kisco, New York

Cal Ashby Marlin, 212
January 1, 1930
Humboldt, Kansas

Fred Joseph Maroon, 58
September 29, 1924
New Brunswick, New Jersey

Lynn Morley Martin, 71
December 26, 1939
Chicago, Illinois

Alexander Morgan Mason, 108
June 26, 1955
Los Angeles, California

Charles McCurdy Mathias, Jr., 201
July 24, 1922
Frederick, Maryland

Sarah Newcomb McClendon, 148
July 8, 1910
Tyler, Texas

Peter McCoy, 58
October 25, 1941
Los Angeles, California

Robert Dane McFarland, 89
December 1, 1938
Burnet, Texas

Robert Carl McFarlane, 73
July 12, 1937
Washington, District of Columbia

John Joseph McLaughlin, 114
March 29, 1927
Providence, Rhode Island

Diana Dicken McLellan, 105
September 22, 1937
Leicester, England

Wallace William McNamee, 93
November 29, 1932
Harrisonburg, Virginia

Melville Peter McPherson, 116
October 27, 1940
Grand Rapids, Michigan

Edwin Meese III, 40
December 2, 1931
Oakland, California

Philip Merrill, 60
April 28, 1934
Baltimore, Maryland

Major Peter Todd Metzger, 140
July 5, 1947
Washington, District of Columbia

Robert Henry Michel, 54
March 2, 1923
Peoria, Illinois

James Clifford Miller III, 188
June 25, 1942
Atlanta, Georgia

Loye Wheat Miller, Jr., 180
March 20, 1930
Knoxville, Tennessee

Roddey Earl Mims, 86
October 26, 1935
Aransas Pass, Texas
Died 1982

Andrea Mitchell, 107
October 30, 1946
New York, New York

Set Charles Momjian, 151
April 9, 1930
Atlantic City, New Jersey

Gillespie V. (Sonny) Montgomery, 71
August 5, 1920
Meridian, Mississippi

Jack Moseley, 103
June 21, 1931
Birmingham, Alabama

Admiral Daniel Joseph Murphy, 178
March 24, 1922
Brooklyn, New York

Alan Curtis Nelson, 206
October 18, 1933
Oakland, California

John Howard Nelson, 99
October 11, 1929
Talladega, Alabama

Paul Henry Nitze, 203
January 16, 1907
Amherst, Massachusetts

Franklyn Curran Nofziger, 63
June 8, 1924
Bakersfield, California

Robert David Novak, 52
February 26, 1931
Joliet, Illinois

Sam Augustus Nunn, 76
September 8, 1938
Perry, Georgia

Sandra Day O'Connor, 43
March 26, 1930
El Paso, Texas

M. B. Oglesby, Jr., 143
October 1, 1942
Flora, Illinois

Yoichi Robert Okamoto, 196
July 3, 1915
Yonkers, New York

Yoshio Okawara, 56
February 5, 1919
Gunma, Japan

Jeremia Aloysius O'Leary, Jr., 152
November 29, 1919
Washington, District of Columbia

Patrick Bruce Oliphant, 192
July 24, 1935
Adelaide, Australia

Thomas Philip (Tip) O'Neill, Jr., 36
December 9, 1912
Cambridge, Massachusetts

Verne Orr, 189
November 12, 1916
Des Moines, Iowa

Katherine Davalos Ortega, 207
July 16, 1934
Tularosa, New Mexico

Kathleen Osborne, 150
December 4, 1943
Sacramento, California

Robert William Packwood, 200
June 11, 1932
Portland, Oregon

Clarence McLane Pendleton, Jr., 31
November 10, 1930
Louisville, Kentucky

Claude Denson Pepper, 67
September 8, 1900
Dudleyville, Alabama

Charles Harting Percy, 97
September 27, 1919
Pensacola, Florida

Martin Peretz, 58
July 30, 1939
New York, New York

James Jarrell Pickle, 169
October 11, 1913
Roscoe, Texas

Samuel Riley Pierce, Jr., 175
September 8, 1922
Glencove, New York

Milton Homer Pitts, 151
July 4, 1919
Greenville, South Carolina

William Plante, 150
January 14, 1938
Chicago, Illinois

Rear Admiral John Marlan Poindexter, 170
August 12, 1936
Washington, District of Columbia

Donna Kolnik Pope, 206
October 15, 1931
Cleveland, Ohio

Roger Blaine Porter, 180
June 19, 1946
Provo, Utah

Howell Hiram Raines, 214
February 5, 1943
Birmingham, Alabama

Jennings Randolph, 218
March 8, 1902
Salem, West Virginia

Maureen Elizabeth Reagan, 205
January 4, 1941
Los Angeles, California

Ronald Wilson Reagan, 38
February 6, 1911
Tampico, Illinois

Joseph Verner Reed, Jr., 157
December 17, 1937
New York, New York

Donald Thomas Regan, 82
December 21, 1918
Cambridge, Massachusetts

Dean Francis Reynolds, 88
August 17, 1948
East Chicago, Indiana

Sidney Dillon Ripley, Jr., 81
September 20, 1913
New York, New York

Nancy J. Risque, 136
April 14, 1946
Paris, France

Bob John Robison, 124
February 5, 1923
Burkeburnett, Texas

John Francis William Rogers, 156
April 15, 1956
Geneva, New York

Edward John Rollins, Jr., 98
March 19, 1943
Boston, Massachusetts

Selwa Showker Roosevelt, 211
January 13, 1929
Kingsport, Tennessee

James Scott Rosebush, 58
June 1, 1949
Flint, Michigan

Meir Rosenne, 103
February 19, 1931
Iase, Rumania

Daniel Rostenkowski, 127
January 2, 1928
Chicago, Illinois

William Victor Roth, Jr., 199
July 22, 1921
Great Falls, Montana

Larry Alan Rubinstein, 213
December 9, 1953
Cleveland, Ohio

William Doyle Ruckelshaus, 194
July 24, 1932
Indianapolis, Indiana

Colonel Robert Earl Ruddick, 65
October 6, 1940
Muncie, Indiana

Daniel August Ruge, M.D., 46
May 13, 1917
Murdock, Nebraska

Donald Henry Rumsfeld, 177
July 9, 1932
Chicago, Illinois

Mark Russell, 187
August 23, 1932
Buffalo, New York

Frederick Joseph Ryan, Jr., 155
April 12, 1955
Tampa, Florida

William Lewis Safire, 100
December 17, 1929
New York, New York

Henry Salvatori, 181
March 28, 1901
Rome, Italy

Maureen Louise Santini, 219
December 31, 1948
Hancock, Michigan

Gary Francis Schuster, 184
January 26, 1942
Detroit, Michigan

Richard Schultz Schweiker, 191
June 1, 1926
Norristown, Pennsylvania

Rex Wayne Scouten, 205
September 16, 1924
Snover, Michigan

Brent Scowcroft, 105
March 19, 1925
Ogden, Utah

Eddie Serano, 217
September 12, 1927
Gapan, Philippines

George Pratt Shultz, 39
December 13, 1920
New York, New York

Hugh Swanson Sidey, 118
September 3, 1927
Greenfield, Iowa

The Honorable William Edward Simon, 46
November 27, 1927
Paterson, New Jersey

General John William Vessey, Jr., 130
June 29, 1922
Minneapolis, Minnesota

Richard Vigurie, 163
September 23, 1933
Golden Acres, Texas

Charles Harding Violette, 212
February 9, 1941
Robertson County, Tennessee

Paul Adolph Volcker, 101
September 5, 1927
Cape May, New Jersey

William Von Raab, 157
January 26, 1942
New Rochelle, New York

Diana Hardin Walker, 196
January 20, 1942
Washington, District of Columbia

Christopher Wallace, 98
October 12, 1947
Chicago, Illinois

Frederick Ward, 196
July 16, 1935
Huntsville, Alabama

Robert Mark Warner, 112
June 28, 1927
Montrose, Colorado

Admiral James David Watkins, 131
March 7, 1927
Alhambra, California

James Gaius Watt, 146
January 31, 1938
Lusk, Wyoming

William Hedgecock Webster, 121
March 6, 1924
Saint Louis, Missouri

Lowell Palmer Weicker, Jr., 144
May 16, 1931
Paris, France

Mark David Weinberg, 87
April 26, 1957
Cleveland, Ohio

Caspar Willard Weinberger, 32
August 18, 1917
San Francisco, California

Steven Roger Weisman, 94
November 10, 1946
Los Angeles, California

Faith Ryan Whittlesey, 164
February 21, 1939
Jersey City, New Jersey

Charles Z. Wick, 110
October 12, 1917
Cleveland, Ohio

General John Adams Wickham, Jr., 131
June 25, 1928
Dobbs Ferry, New York

George Frederick Will, 8
May 4, 1941
Champagne-Urbana, Illinois

Lieutenant General James Arthur Williams, 105
March 29, 1932
Paterson, New Jersey

Peter Barton Wilson, 172
August 23, 1933
Lake Forest, Illinois

William Albert Wilson, 89
November 3, 1914
Los Angeles, California

Richard Bitner Wirthlin, 113
March 15, 1931
Salt Lake City, Utah

Judy Woodruff, 107
November 20, 1946
Tulsa, Oklahoma

James Claude Wright, Jr., 197
December 22, 1922
Fort Worth, Texas

Sir Oliver Wright, 137
March 6, 1921
London, England

Walter Bigelow Wriston, 214
August 3, 1919
Middletown, Connecticut

Efrem Zimbalist, Jr., 94
November 30, 1918
New York, New York

Jerome Robert Zipkin, 83
December 18, 1916
New York, New York